Food in a Minute

Recipes from the Popular TV Series

with
Allyson Gofton

contents

PENGUIN BOOKS

Penguin Books (NZ) Ltd, cnr Airborne and Rosedale Roads,
Albany, Auckland 1310, New Zealand

Penguin Books Ltd, 27 Wrights Lane, London W8 5TZ, England

Penguin Putnam Inc, 375 Hudson Street,
New York, NY 10014, United States

Penguin Books Australia Ltd, 487 Maroondah Highway,
Ringwood, Australia 3134

Penguin Books Canada Ltd, 10 Alcorn Avenue,
Toronto, Ontario, Canada M4V 3B2

Penguin Books (South Africa) Pty Ltd, 4 Pallinghurst Road,
Parktown, Johannesburg 2193, South Africa

Penguin Books India (P) Ltd, 11, Community Centre,
Panchsheel Park, New Delhi 110 017, India

Penguin Books Ltd, Registered Offices:
Harmondsworth, Middlesex, England

First published by Penguin Books (NZ) Ltd
under the Viking imprint, 1997
Reprinted 1997 (four times), 1998 (twice)
This edition first published by
Penguin Books (NZ) Ltd, 1999

1 2 3 4 5 6 7 8 9 10

Photography by Alan Gillard and Nick Tresidder

Designed by Hot House Design Group, Auckland

Printed by Wyatt and Wilson Print, Christchurch

introduction

The team at Wattie's.

Food in a Minute all began back in June 1995 when Mike O'Sullivan, CEO of Channel i, rang me to see if we could get together on an idea he had. Mike saw the opportunity for someone to present quick meal ideas which would be flavoursome, healthy and low-cost, in the form of a programmette just before the news — appointment viewing.

Mike wanted me to be the personality; the person to hang the name of 'Food in a Minute' on. With a presentation kit in hand, off he went to see a number of possible sponsors who would value this new approach. John Macdonald and his team at Wattie's loved the *Food in a Minute* idea and took it on board with gusto.

With assistance from Fisher and Paykel (who supplied the kitchen appliances) Buttermark and New Zealand Cheese, TVNZ (providers of a great time slot), *Next* magazine (publishers of the recipes), and a small talented cast and crew, we put it all together.

The success was beyond all our imaginings. We knew people were stretched for time to prepare meals, but never did we think that so many of you would tune in every night to see the next idea, be it brunch, lunch, dinner, desserts or snacks.

The production of each *Food in a Minute* programmette is a team effort. We begin each ten-episode filming session with a team meeting at the Wattie's offices to discuss the ideas I would like to present, the products the managers would like to see used, and the season's requirements — what the people out there need to know or have in, say, winter.

Then, later on, I sit down in my rather eclectic kitchen, armed with a glass of wine and the list of requirements. I juggle everything around, and end up collating a collection of about 30 meal ideas.

Next the Wattie's team discusses the ideas and decides on a shortlist of ten. Then it's back to the kitchen where each recipe is tested, probably two to three times. Some, like Tuscan Chicken, can take five testings until I get it just right.

Simplicity is the key and this is definitely vital during our one-minute time-frame on TV.

With recipes approved I prepare the scripts. These have set introductions and 'outro's' in them, but after filming over 70 programmettes I don't think I have ever stuck to the scripts once — often to Wattie's amusement and occasional frustration!

Once all the scripts are approved (about four weeks' work), the main production team gets together for a team meeting.

There's Colin Follas, owner of Tiger Films, the production company, Mike O'Sullivan, the series creator and executive producer, me, the cook, Viv Kerr, the chief coordinator from Wattie's, and Rob McLaughlin, director extraordinaire, who constantly comes up with new angles to ensure that it looks different every time. It's about here that the *Food in a Minute* programmettes begin to come to life.

Rob — director extraordinaire.

As an aside, it's worth mentioning that after working together for over a year the team has become something of a mini Coronation Street series in itself. We catch up on each other's lives every eight weeks, and over a year it means we can piece together — without the fine detail — what's been happening to each of us.

When we began, the producer Rob and his fab wife Michelle were looking for a section to build a house on. By the time of the second series they'd found a section, then disagreed with the council and seller over water and sewerage installation costs (series 3), approved the architect's plans (series 4), moved to Michelle's grandmother's to live in-between time (series 5), and began to build (series 6) — I remember quite clearly when

the roof went on as it was raining and Rob would check progress during his lunch-hours. Finally it was the big 'move in' with the floorboards being polished, which forced Rob and Michelle to live in the hallway with no kitchen and so each night we'd send Rob home with food from the shoot for dinner (series 7). Now they're in and we are all waiting for our invite to dinner!

Filming follows the production meeting — a whole week of hard work mixed with lots of fun. Our shoot mornings begin with coffee made by the production assistant (who records timings for the editor Phil) to wake us up.

Make-up starts early, with curlers and thick goop on the face that looks 'oh-so-glam' by the end of the day. The 'Allyson look' is carefully designed and guarded by Suzanne Arts, make-up artist and stylist. Suzanne and I have normally been shopping by this time to find the clothes for each series. We look for colours and styles that are in season, but nothing too ritzy — that's not really my style.

With make-up on and a wide-awake crew in place the filming starts. Out in the second kitchen is my assistant. Over the time I've had two fabulous ladies work with me. One was Sarah-Jane Gillies who, by series 4, when she was heavy with her second child, farewelled us all to become a full-time mum. (By series 7, Poppy-May, then 5 weeks old, paid us a visit. This completely stopped filming as we took time out to 'ooh' and 'aah' over her.)

Suzanne – make-up starts early.

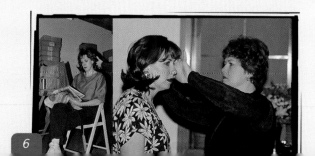

Sarah-Jane and Poppy-May.

My assistant now is Anna Richards. Anna has everything prepared for me; without her I'd be lost. The food is purchased, chopped, sliced or diced — ready for each session. All the props have been hired, a process often involving days of battling traffic and scouring shops to find the right plates and accessories for each meal, also the right background, crockery, matching cutlery and glassware. Not to mention flowers for the set and other props I bring from home.

So with the food on the set, the lights go on and the camera rolls. I am lucky to work with the talents of Rhys Duncan and Warwick Wrigley on camera; both have their own styles and bring new thoughts to each programmette. On lighting

Anna – making sure that the food looks just right.

is Adrian Greshof from South Africa, and even if they do hold the World Cup we really like him. I often wonder what Ado is up to, but it will turn out that he's searching as usual for perfection with the right slash of light in the background or on the food.

Assistant cameraman Taks (left) and Rhys.

Lighting by Adrian.

I'm wired for sound by Bernie Wright, who once had the task of recording sound while we put up with the construction of 23 townhouses right across the road. The builders finished during series 7 (a bit like Rob's house), and on many occasions we bribed them with hot muffins or whatever we had been cooking to get them to turn all their equipment off while we filmed the outro!

Each programmette takes us about half a day to film, and so we finish just in time for lunch or to catch the hideous Auckland traffic home! And of course there's no wrapping up without eating the food. The crew are my greatest critics and we can measure the success of each dish by what's left!

Soundman Bernie, assisted here by Warwick.

After a week, and with the crew departed, Anna and I take to the kitchen again with photographers Alan Gillard or Nick Tresidder to re-cook everything for the stills photography. The shots are then used with the recipes in *Next* magazine. By now I know all the recipes off by heart!

And it doesn't really finish there. The tapes have winged their way to Phil England at Tiger Films to be edited and cut to a one-minute duration. Phil only gets to drool over the food, there's no tasting at his end.

With a rough cut done, the scripts are corrected and we put the voice down for the recipe instructions. Both Rob and Neil Newcombe do a little fine-tuning here. The technology is so amazing; a breath is removed here or there, a sizzle is added, or a boiling noise increased and – *voila!* – it's all over bar sending the tapes to TVNZ.

Stills photographer Alan Gillard.

Now, in all of this there's one person who's not paid or officially on the crew, but without him it would be much harder — and that's Warwick Kiely, husband of much greater patience and tolerance than you can imagine, chief taste-tester, gaffer for all the things I forget (and that's lots) and my pick-me-up when it's all too much. He has to be mentioned or otherwise I'll be in big trouble next time I forget something!

There are two other people who also deserve a big thank-you: Steve Barnett, my editor, and John Dick, GM of the Carlton Hotel. John allows me time off from my full-time job as public relations manager and supports me all the way with *Food in a Minute*, for which I am very grateful.

With 70 meal programmettes under our belt the series looks set to continue with another 70 ideas being developed, thanks to Wattie's.

In this first book I have included recipes from the first year, interspersed with tips and ideas. I hope that you'll enjoy them all over again.

On the set (left to right): Taks, Rob and Mike.

allyson Gotton.

what I use

Cooking is supposed to be fun and the finished product should taste great. Here's a list of some of the things I use on Food in a Minute that I believe help achieve this result.

Butter:
I am a butter fan; I prefer its taste. Use clarified butter for pan frying; creamery and unsalted for baking.

Oil:
I use olive oil where I can. It is expensive but for, say, cooking onions, you can use a light olive oil. For dishes where you will taste the difference, like in a salad, use virgin.

Fresh herbs:
These make all the difference to a dish. I have the basics like parsley, thyme, chives and mint in my garden; otherwise I buy as I need from the supermarket.

Sharp knives:
These are essential for both easy preparation and safety. If you plan to buy knives, invest in quality products as you will have them forever. You should have a paring knife, a cook's knife and a medium-sized all-purpose knife.

A garlic set:
This should include a garlic board to chop garlic on separately (so you do not taint your chopping board with garlic) and a garlic tube peeler that will quickly remove the skin from your cloves of garlic.

A decent sized chopping board:
You will need one that will hold a good amount of food on top. Buy a wooden one; look after it well and it will last you a lifetime. I purchased my large kauri board over ten years ago. It was a great investment.

A set of measuring cups and spoons:
As well as these essential items you could invest in a set of scales to take away the guesswork. A food processor is also useful; you should look for a solid machine that will take a heavy strain. I also have a Moulinex mini whizz which is about a one-cup sized chopper — I'd be lost without it for parsley and small amounts of food.

Seasoning:
I use freshly ground black pepper and Maldon sea salt, both of which I couldn't do without at home.

Frying pan:
For pan frying, a heavy-based, non-stick frying pan with a lid (so you can simmer, say, a casserole on top of the stove) is an all-purpose wonder. On the set we have used predominantly Scanpan equipment which works well.

Saucepans:
With pasta being so fashionable, invest in a large stock pot for cooking pasta. Buy as good a quality saucepan range as you can, preferably with a thick copper base, and buy to suit your requirements. Don't worry about buying a complete set from the same manufacturer; they may not make all the sizes you want.

Pyrex bowls:
You can't beat a selection of pyrex bowls. They have multiple uses — you can beat mixtures in them, use them to store food in, and cook with them in the microwave.

Kitchen utensils:
Fashionable utensils are everywhere. Don't be misled by designer items, get the most practical ones. I find that the best fish slices and holed mixing spoons are available in supermarkets at half the price of those in specialty shops.

Bake-ware:
My bake-ware is mainly non-stick, but I still grease everything to ensure I never scratch the non-stick lining. Once it is scratched, food will stick.

My last piece of advice is to look around when you purchase expensive kitchen equipment. Buy the best quality you can afford, so that your purchase is a once-only investment.

The photographer's polaroids are only for the record and so occasionally we ham it up. Each outfit is specially chosen for its colour or style to match the food idea or the crockery and props – so that everything goes together.

light meals

snacks

nibbles

quick mussel chowder

Adding freshly-cooked mussels to a can of Pumpkin and Orange Soup was a real hit with the production team when we filmed this recipe. You could use other Wattie's soups such as Hearty Minestrone, Seafood Bisque or Spicy Tomato and Vegetable.

Ingredients

16 - 20 fresh mussels in shell

1 cup water

1 bayleaf

dash of oil

2 stalks celery, trimmed and finely diced

1 carrot, peeled and finely diced

½ leek or 1 small onion, finely diced

1 tsp curry powder

2 x 560 gram cans **Wattie's Pumpkin and Orange Soup**

sour cream and chopped parsley to garnish

Method

1   Discard any mussels that are open. Scrub the mussels and remove the beards. Heat the water and bayleaf in a saucepan until boiling rapidly. Add the mussels, cover and boil for 5 minutes. Drain the mussels in a colander and allow to cool; set aside.

2   In a saucepan heat the dash of oil and gently cook the celery, carrot, leek or onion and curry powder for about 3-5 minutes until softened but not browned.

3   Stir in the two cans of soup and bring to a simmer. Reduce heat but do not boil.

4   Discard any mussels that have not opened this time. Remove the meat from the shells of the ones that have, and chop roughly. Add the mussels to the soup and warm through.

5   Ladle into warm soup bowls and garnish with a dollop of sour cream and parsley.

If your cellphone rings during filming, there's a penalty system in which it's your shout for chocolate or muffins that day: inevitably the phone rings right in the middle of a perfect take. On this occasion, cameraman Rhys Duncan is caught out.

Preparation Time: 10 minutes
Cooking Time: 15 minutes
Serves 4

Cook's tip

Another idea for Wattie's Pumpkin and Orange Soup is to add a well drained can of **Wattie's Whole Kernel Corn** and ¼ cup chopped parsley. Corn and pumpkin go together really well.

Preparation Time: 5 minutes
Cooking Time: 15-20 minutes
Serves 6 as nibbles

Cook's tip

For a fuller cheese flavour use
1 cup grated Cheddar cheese and
½ cup grated Parmesan or Romano
cheese. I also like to add chopped
jalepeno peppers for extra zing.
The chilli peppers come mild to
hot, fresh or bottled, and are
available in supermarkets.

*Director Rob McLaughlin on set with me, talking over
how best to approach the next part of filming.*

mexican
cheese dip with
zestie potatoes

As cheese lovers, this hot Mexican cheese dip is a real favourite in our house. We enjoy it with BBQs in summer or with drinks by the fire in winter. I've been making it for years, so it was great when I had the opportunity to present it on Food in a Minute.

Ingredients

1 tblsp oil

2 spring onions, minced or finely chopped

2 tsp ground cumin

1 tsp ground coriander

*300 gram can **Wattie's Tomato Salsa***

½ x 250 gram tub cream cheese

¼ cup cream

1½ cups grated tasty Cheddar cheese

1 tblsp cornflour

pepper to season

*1 packet **Wattie's Extra Mild Zesties** (crispy coated potatoes wedges)*

Method

1 Heat the oil in a saucepan and cook the spring onions, cumin and coriander for 2-3 minutes until quite fragrant.

2 Add the tomato salsa to the saucepan with the cream cheese and stir until melted.

3 Add the cream, grated cheese and cornflour. Allow to cook over a very low heat, stirring all the time until thickened and hot. Season with pepper.

4 Place the potato zesties on a baking tray and cook according to the directions on the back of the packet.

5 Serve the cheese dip in a large bowl with the zesties.

soup *under* crispy pastry topping

A can of soup can easily be jazzed up by cooking it under a pastry top. There's a list of variations opposite giving ideas on how to increase the flavour of your soup without very much effort.

Ingredients

425 gram **Wattie's Concentrated Soup,** of your choice

2 sheets pre-rolled puff pastry

milk to glaze

Method

1 Make up the soup according to the directions on the back of the soup can in a heat-proof microwave jug. I tend to prefer to make the soups with a whole can of milk; that way I include more calcium in my diet — but it's up to you.

2 Heat on high power (100%) in the microwave for 2 minutes. If you do not have a microwave, warm the soup through in a saucepan until the soup is luke-warm. You should just take the chill off the soup.

3 Take 4 all-purpose, very sturdy kitchen cups that will take the heat of an oven. Turn them upside-down on the sheets of pastry and cut a circle that is 1 cm larger than that of the cup rim.

4 Place the cups on a baking tray and fill with equal quantities of soup.

5 Cover each cup with the pastry topping and press firmly onto the outside edge of the cup. Use any left-over pieces of pastry to decorate the pastry tops with. Brush with milk to glaze.

6 Bake at 220°C for 12-15 minutes until the pastry is golden and well-risen.

7 Carefully transfer the soups to the saucer to serve. Crack through the pastry to the steaming hot soup. Delicious!

Variations

Add chunks of ham to Pumpkin or Pumpkin and Orange Soup.

Add chopped surimi (crabmeat) to Seafood Bisque.

Lots of chopped chives will add new flavour to Creamy Asparagus Soup.

Add a few finely sliced field mushrooms to a can of Mushroom Soup and a dollop of sour cream to every serving.

Fresh herbs like parsley, thyme and chives, along with a few chopped olives, will do wonders for Hearty Minestrone Soup.

Make the concentrated soups up with ¾ milk and ¼ cream for extra richness.

If your a blue cheese lover, crumble a little blue cheese into the Creamy Asparagus Soup; it's a wonderful partnership.

Preparation Time: 5 minutes
Cooking Time: 12-15 minutes
Serves 4

Cook's tip

Always keep butter in the butter conditioner to ensure it stays at the right temperature for easy and convenient use.

Preparation Time: 15 minutes
Cooking Time: 20 minutes
Serves 4

Cook's tip

The same filling mixture can
be used to make mini pies.

cheese &
chilli con carne tart

A good, old fashioned scone dough can be used as the base for many dishes, even deep dish pizzas. This Chilli Con Carne Tart is perfect for those 'lazy days' kind of meals.

Ingredients

2 cups self-raising flour

25 grams butter

¾ cup grated tasty Cheddar cheese

2 tblsp chopped fresh thyme or parsley

¾ cup milk

425 gram can **Wattie's Chilli Con Carne**

1 courgette, trimmed and grated

2 tblsp finely chopped black olives (optional)

milk to glaze

½ cup grated Cheddar cheese for topping

Method

1. Sift the flour into a bowl and rub in the butter until the mixture resembles fine crumbs. Stir in the cheese and thyme or parsley.

2. Stir in the milk to form a soft dough and knead lightly until smooth.

3. Roll the dough out on a floured board to about a 30 cm diameter circle.

4. Place the dough over the base and sides of a 24 cm flan or cake tin allowing the edges to overhang.

5. Combine the chilli con carne, courgettes and olives and pile into the scone-lined tin.

6. Flip the edges over and brush with milk to glaze. Sprinkle the second measure of grated cheese over the top.

7. Bake at 200°C for 20 minutes, or until hot and golden.

spicy plum pork spareribs

The marinade for these spareribs is incredibly easy and the final taste really 'more-ish'. I prefer to use pork fingers to spareribs, but you need to trim off any excess fat with the fingers. The marinade could also work well for chicken drumsticks, wings, lamb chops or beef spareribs. Spareribs are wonderfully messy, so have plenty of serviettes and a finger bowl standing by.

Ingredients

2 kg pork spareribs

425 gram can **Wattie's Spicy Plum Stir Fry Sauce**

¼ cup sweet sherry

Method

1 Cut down between the bones of the spareribs and place the spareribs in a large shallow dish.

2 Puree the contents of the spicy plum sauce in a blender or processor with the sherry.

3 Pour over the spareribs and toss well to coat evenly. Cover, refrigerate and leave overnight or for at least 4 hours to marinate.

4 Place on a rack above a foil-lined tray. Bake at 190°C for 1-1¼ hours or until the spareribs are well cooked and crispy.

Preparation Time: 10 minutes
Cooking Time: 1-1¼ hours
Serves 6

Cook's tip

As the marinade has sugar in it, I like to line the tray they're cooked on with foil. It's easier to clean up - all you have to do is peel it off and throw it away. Saves scrubbing!

baked bean *hash*

If you're looking for something rather outrageous for a weekend breakfast or brunch, then try this Baked Bean Hash. It's just the thing and I'm sure this will be a hit with those younger members of your home.

Ingredients

360 gram packet **Wattie's Hash Browns**

425 gram can **Wattie's Baked Beans**

4 eggs

4 rashers bacon

¾ cup grated Edam cheese (optional)

freshly ground black pepper to season (optional)

chopped parsley to garnish (optional)

Method

1 Place the hash browns in the base of a 16 cm x 26 cm baking dish, trimming where necessary.

2 Pour over the baked beans and even out.

3 Beat the eggs together and pour over the top of the baked beans.

4 Finely slice the bacon and sprinkle on top of the eggs. Sprinkle over the cheese if using and season with pepper, if wished.

5 Bake at 200°C at the top of the oven for 30 minutes until set. Stand for 2 minutes before serving. Sprinkle with the chopped parsley if using. Serve in wedges.

Preparation Time: 5 minutes
Cooking Time: 30 minutes
Serves 4

Preparation Time: 30 minutes
Serves 5-6

Cook's tip

Broad beans are the ugly duckling
of beans. Once peeled they're
delicate, sweet and tender. I
always have a packet on hand in
the freezer to add to casseroles,
soups or salads. Take another
look at them, as broad beans are
definitely worth it.

*Eggs should be stored in the refrigerator in the egg stand to ensure long
shelf life. Stand the eggs with the pointed end downwards, the opposite
way to which you buy them. On the set we used an antique egg stand for
propping. It would have been used to hold eggs in the larder before the
invention of the refrigerator.*

french salad

One of my favourite ways of eating over summer is to enjoy a meal in one salad and this French Salad is a variation of the classic Niçoise salad. It is truly delicious and ideal to have with friends or family. All you need are large bowls of delicious fresh bread to accompany the salad and a nice chilled white wine.

Ingredients

500 gram packet **Wattie's Broad Beans** (optional)

½ x 500 gram packet **Wattie's Frozen Whole Baby Beans**

1 lettuce (iceburg)

4 tomatoes, cut into eighths

10 cooked baby potatoes, halved

4 hard-boiled eggs

185 gram can **Wattie's Tuna in Spring Water**

12 black olives (optional)

Dressing

½ cup **Wattie's Mayonnaise**

¼ cup chopped fresh herbs

2 tblsp water

Method

1 Blanch the broad and baby beans in boiling water for 2 minutes. Refresh in cold water, drain well. Peel the broad beans.

2 Wash and drain the lettuce. Cut into large pieces and arrange on a large platter.

3 Sprinkle over half the whole baby and broad beans. Top with the tomatoes and potatoes.

4 Halve the hard-boiled eggs and place on top. Sprinkle over the remaining whole baby and broad beans.

5 Drain the tuna and place pieces over the top of the salad. Lastly sprinkle over the olives.

Dressing
Blend all the dressing ingredients together until smooth and spoon over just before serving.

corn & *asparagus* tart

Summer eating is all about light foods, and this simple corn and asparagus tart is ideal hot or cold for a picnic. It's also ideal for a casual meal in winter, served with extra vegetables and crusty bread rolls.

Ingredients

2 sheets pre-rolled savoury pastry

3 eggs

3 spring onions, trimmed and finely chopped

¾ cup grated Cheddar cheese

½ cup cream

1 cup milk

*425 gram can **Wattie's Mexi-corn**, well drained*

*½ x 340 gram can **Wattie's Asparagus Spears**, well drained*

Method

1 Roll the pastry sheets out together, large enough to fit the base and sides of a 24 cm flan tin. Bake blind at 200°C for 15 minutes. See South of the Border Pie, page 44.

2 In a bowl mix together the eggs, spring onions, ½ cup of the grated Cheddar cheese, cream, milk, and Mexi-corn. Remove the baking blind material from the tin and pour in the filling.

3 Arrange the asparagus spears on top and sprinkle over the remaining ¼ cup grated Cheddar cheese.

4 Bake at 180°C for about 40 minutes until the filling is golden and set.

Preparation Time: 15 minutes
Cooking Time: 55 minutes
Serves 6

Cook's tip

Open cans of asparagus spears upside-down and then gently turn the spears out into a sieve to strain. This way you won't break the spears up more than you need to and you'll get perfect tips every time.

s m o k e d
chicken pizza

Pizzas make great fast meals and combined here with smoked chicken the final product is rather delicious.

Ingredients

¼ cup **Wattie's Italian Seasoned Tomato Puree**

27 cm diameter pre-cooked pizza base

1 red pepper, halved and deseeded

1 **Tegel Smoked Chicken Breast**, finely sliced

2 medium tomatoes, finely sliced

1 tblsp chopped fresh oregano or 1 tsp dried

1 cup grated Mozarella or Edam cheese

12-18 black or stuffed green olives

Method

1 Spread the pizza base with the Italian seasoned tomato puree. Take the filling right out to the edge of the pizza.

2 Finely dice one half of the red pepper and slice the second half. Sprinkle the diced pepper over the tomato puree. Arrange the sliced smoked chicken and tomato slices on top and sprinkle with oregano.

3 Sprinkle over the grated Mozarella or Edam cheese. Arrange the red pepper slices on top of the cheese in a criss cross diamond pattern. Fill the diamonds with olives.

4 Bake at 220°C for about 15-20 minutes until the pizza is hot and golden. Serve with a crisp green salad.

Preparation Time: 10 minutes
Cooking Time: 20 minutes
Serves 4

Cook's tip

Freeze any leftover **Wattie's Italian Seasoned Tomato Puree** in ice cube trays. Once frozen, transfer to a bag and seal. The cubes can be added to a sauce, gravy, soup or casserole.

mexican
stuffed peppers

In summer when peppers are in abundance and their price has fallen, it's time to enjoy a pepper overload. They're sweet and delicious and make a great vehicle for holding stuffing made from rice, Wattie's Bean Salsa and other summer ingredients. On Food in a Minute, these peppers had their tops removed to be stuffed, but here in the picture I have cut them in half like boats – you can choose which way you prefer.

Ingredients

½ cup white rice

4 large red peppers (or 6 medium)

2 spring onions, finely chopped

310 gram can **Wattie's Whole Kernel Corn**, well drained

300 gram can **Wattie's Bean Salsa**

2 tomatoes, finely chopped

2 - 4 tblsp chopped parsley

salt and pepper to season

¼ cup grated Cheddar cheese

Method

1 Cook the white rice in boiling salted water for 10 minutes. Drain well.

2 Cut the tops off the peppers. Remove the stem, core and seeds from inside. Finely chop any fleshy parts of the pepper tops and set aside. Trim the bases of each pepper so that they stand up straight.

3 In a bowl blend together the rice, chopped peppers, spring onions, drained corn and bean salsa, tomatoes and parsley and, if wished, season with salt and pepper.

4 Fill the peppers with the mixture and top with cheese. Place in a baking dish that will hold the peppers and pour ¼ cup water into the bottom. Bake at 190°C for 35-40 minutes, until the red peppers are soft when pierced with a skewer.

Preparation Time: 10 minutes
Cooking Time: 50 minutes
Makes 4

Make-up artist Sue Arts does 'finals' before we take the 'outro' to one of the programmettes. Sue has to ensure that how I looked when I said hello is still the same four hours later after cooking over steam and standing under lights. A polaroid is normally taken at the beginning to ensure we get it right at the outro.

Cook's tip

Brown rice would make a wonderfully nutty change to white rice. You would need to cook brown rice for 35 minutes before mixing it with other ingredients.

mixed bean falafels
with minted yoghurt

Falafels or chick pea patties make a wonderful vegetarian meal or nibble at a party. Normally they're prepared from chick peas and tahini or sesame paste, but in this recipe I used a mixture of Craig's prepared beans; that cuts the preparation time dramatically. For a dip, arrange the falafels on a platter with yoghurt sauce in the centre. For a main course serve them with tabbouleh, pita breads, diced tomatoes and diced cucumber tossed in extra minted yoghurt.

Ingredients

*300 gram can **Craig's Chick Peas** in brine, well drained*

*425 gram can **Craig's Four Bean Mix** in brine, well drained*

½ cup fresh chopped parsley

3-4 cloves garlic, crushed and peeled

1 onion, peeled and chopped

1 tsp ground cumin

2 tsp ground coriander

3 tblsp flour

salt and pepper to season

clarified butter or oil to pan fry in

Method

1 Put all ingredients up to the clarified butter into a food processor and pulse to form a smooth paste.

2 Take tablespoonful-lots of the mixture and roll into balls and flatten into patties.

3 Heat the clarified butter or oil in a frying pan and cook the bean patties for about 5 minutes on each side over a moderate heat until golden.

4 Serve with minted yoghurt.

Minted Yoghurt
Mix together 2 tblsp chopped fresh mint with ½ cup unsweetened natural yoghurt.

Preparation Time: 10 minutes
Cooking Time: 10 minutes
Makes 12

w i n t e r
frittata

Frittata is an Italian omelet, but is quite different in style from the traditional French omelet. It's thick with fillings, cooked over a low heat and cooked on both sides (we baked ours though). Frittata is served hot or cold and in wedges, so after all of that, it's probably not much like an omelet at all!

Ingredients

2 tblsp oil

3 potatoes, washed and evenly diced

100 grams bacon or ham, roughly diced

2 onions, peeled and finely diced

250 gram packet **Wattie's Frozen Chopped Spinach**, *defrosted*

1 cup diced cheese (feta, blue or other favourites)

6 eggs

Method

1 Heat the oil in a large oven-proof frying pan. Add the potatoes, bacon or ham, and onion and cook over a low to moderate heat for 15 minutes, stirring occassionally until the potatoes are almost cooked and very golden.

2 Arrange the spinach and cheese evenly over the pan.

3 Beat the eggs together. (You can add a pinch of salt if wished, though with the cheese it's not a requirement.)

4 Cook for about 3-4 minutes on top of the stove and then transfer to a 190°C oven for about 15 minutes, until the frittata is well cooked and firm to the touch. Stand for 5 minutes before turning out to serve. Frittata is great for brunch or lunch with a large bowl of salad or steaming vegetables.

Preparation Time: 10 minutes
Cooking Time: 40 minutes
Serves 6

Preparation Time: 15 minutes
Cooking Time: 10 minutes
Makes 8

Cream style corn does not contain any cream, just a thick sauce loaded with chopped up corn kernels.

Keep ginger on hand to jazz up dishes. Add a little, grated, to a pork casserole, or make mashed kumara fabulous, or transform a chicken or turkey stuffing. Toss with butter over freshly cooked vegetables, add to freshly cooked rice to accompany Chinese, or add to a salad dressing.

kumara &
corn fritters

The team at Wattie's were very keen that I prepared corn fritters on Food in a Minute because they were one of the most requested recipes. We tested this version four times to get it perfect and the final result was devoured by the crew in minutes. The fritters are delicious and great for late breakfast or lunch.

Ingredients

310 gram can **Wattie's Cream Style Corn**

2 tsp finely chopped fresh ginger

2 tblsp chopped fresh herbs (thyme or chives are great here)

½ cup self raising flour

¼ cup milk

1 egg, separated

½ cup roughly mashed cooked cold kumara

butter or oil for pan frying

Method

1 In a bowl mix together the cream style corn, ginger, herbs, self-raising flour, milk and egg yolk.

2 In a clean bowl beat the egg white until stiff. Fold the egg white and kumara into the mixture.

3 Heat a little butter or oil in a non-stick frying pan (the butter helps to crispen the outside of the fritters) and cook large spoonfuls over a low to moderate heat for about three minutes each side. Serve with crispy grilled bacon rashers, grilled tomatoes and a drizzle of golden syrup.

courgette and
pineapple slice

This slice is perfect hot or cold, served with a tomato salad and plenty of crusty bread. It's a different way of using hash browns and it works particularly well.

Ingredients

720 gram packet **Wattie's Onion Hash Browns**

2 cups grated Swiss cheese (or use Gruyere)

2 grated courgettes

4 eggs

432 gram can crushed pineapple, well drained

4 spring onions, trimmed and finely chopped

200 grams ham, finely chopped

pepper to season

Method

1 Line a 23 cm x 29 cm slice tin with foil.

2 Arrange the hash browns over the base, cutting them to fit where necessary.

3 In a food processor put the cheese, courgettes, eggs, pineapple, spring onions and ham and process until well mixed.

4 Pour over the potato hash brown base and level off.

5 Bake at 190°C for 45-55 minutes until firm to the touch and golden. Serve in slices with a tomato salad.

Preparation Time: 10 minutes
Cooking Time: 55 minutes
Serves 6-8

p i t a
pizzas

Pita bread makes the perfect base for pizzas in minute – great for after school snacks, served with a fruit juice or milk drink.

Ingredients

8 pita rounds

2-3 tomatoes, finely sliced

*425 gram can **Wattie's Pizza Spaghetti***

1 cup grated Colby cheese

Extras

Whatever you like: Shaved ham, sliced luncheon, olives, cooked vegetables, salami, leftover cooked meats, finely sliced peppers, spring onions or celery

Method

1 Toast the pita breads on one side by placing them under a hot grill for about 2 minutes.

2 Turn them over and cover the base with 2-3 slices of tomato.

3 Top with a spoonful spaghetti, grated Colby cheese, and ham or bacon (optional).

4 Grill in a hot oven for 5 minutes until the cheese has melted and is golden brown. If you like, add extra filling — whatever is in your fridge.

Preparation Time: 10 minutes
Cooking Time: 5 minutes
Makes 8

Cook's tip

Keep a packet of pita bread in the freezer to have on hand for emergency snack times.

c u r r i e d
tuna fish cakes

*When the programme on these fish cakes went to air, we still had the 0900
number operating and for many weeks this recipe was one of the most requested
recipes. Add herbs such as chopped parsley or chives or garlic chives for
extra flavour.*

Ingredients

4 large potatoes, peeled and
quartered

hearty knob butter

½ onion, finely chopped

1-2 tsp curry powder

425 gram can **Wattie's Tuna in
Spring Water**, well drained

1 egg

clarified butter or oil to pan fry
with

Method

1   Cook the potatoes in boiling salted water for
    about 15 minutes until tender. Drain well and
    mash with the knob of butter.

2   Add the onion and curry powder, and then flake
    in the well drained can of tuna in spring water.
    Add the egg and mix well with a fork, but try to
    keep some largish pieces of tuna in the mixture.

3   Dust your hands with flour and mould the
    mixture into 8 even-sized and shaped patties.

4   Heat the clarified butter in a frying pan and cook
    the tuna cakes for 5 minutes on each side until
    golden and hot through. Serve with grilled
    tomatoes or sliced pineapple and a fresh salad.

Preparation Time: 5 minutes
Cooking Time: 10 minutes
Serves 4-6

Cook's tip

For a different flavour, use
mashed kumara in place of
potatoes and add the grated
rind of an orange.

main courses

r u s s i a n
tuna pie

This tuna pie is based on a Russian koulibiaka, made with salmon and rice. It looked great cooking in the oven on the set, but getting it all into one minute proved to be a heavy task for Phil, the editor who had to somehow make sure you got to see all the steps in just 60 seconds.

Ingredients

½ x 750 gram bag **Wattie's Frozen Rice and Vegetables**

185 gram can **Wattie's Tuna in Oil**, well drained

4 spring onions, finely chopped

½ cup sour cream

¼ cup chopped parsley

1 tsp dried dill

salt and pepper

2 x 400 gram packets frozen puff pastry, defrosted

3 hard-boiled eggs

milk to glaze

Method

1 In a bowl mix together the rice and vegetables with the flaked tuna, spring onions, sour cream, parsley and dill. Season with salt and pepper.

2 Roll the first block of pastry out to a 35 cm x 30 cm rectangle and freehand cut out the shape of a large fish. Place on a baking tray.

3 Spread the filling over the pastry fish base leaving a 1 cm border. Arrange the eggs down the centre. Brush the edges with milk to seal.

4 Roll the second block of pastry out 5 cm wider on all sides, to around 40 cm x 35 cm and place on top, pressing down firmly around the edge. Trim off the excess pastry.

5 Decorate the fish, using a rounded end of a spoon to make scales and using leftover pastry trimmings if wished. Brush with milk to glaze.

6 Bake at 220°C for 25-30 minutes. Serve in slices with steamed winter vegetables, or alongside a crisp salad in summer, with a little extra sour cream.

Preparation Time: 20-30 minutes
Cooking Time: 30 minutes
Serves 6

Cook's tip

If keeping onions in the
refrigerator, make sure that the
onions are well wrapped or
preferably in a lidded container.
Keep well away from dairy
foods in your refrigerator to
ensure the onion does not taint
butter or cream. Onion flavours
will spread throughout your
fridge so keep onions well to
one side and use up quickly.

chicken *paella*

Filming the outros for each programme is always greeted with excitement. It means we (the crew) will get to savour the dish in the next few minutes. While wrapping up filming on this dish, I suggested pouring a splash of sherry over the top before serving. However, with more takes than usual, the paella ended up swimming in the sherry and the crew enjoyed this dish more than normal!

Ingredients

2 double **Tegel chicken breasts**

2-3 tblsp oil

1 onion, peeled and finely diced

3 cloves garlic, crushed, peeled and chopped

1 tsp each mild chilli, turmeric and cumin

1½ cups long grain rice

400 gram can **Wattie's Italian Seasoned Tomatoes**

1 cup water

100 grams finely sliced salami

1 cup **Wattie's Frozen Peas**

¼ cup dry sherry

Method

1   Trim the skin from the chicken breasts and cut the breasts into largish pieces.

2   Heat the oil in a large frying pan, add the chicken pieces and brown quickly over a high heat. Once browned, add the onion, garlic, spices and rice. Cook for 1 minute.

3   Stir in the seasoned tomatoes, water and salami and stir to even out all the ingredients. Cover and lower to a gentle simmer for 20 minutes.

4   Sprinkle over peas, cover and stand for 5 minutes before fluffing up with a fork.

5   Pour over the sherry just before serving. Serve with a medley of autumn vegetables, or with a crisp salad in summer.

Preparation Time: 15 minutes
Cooking Time: 30 minutes
Serves 4

To prepare garlic quickly, crush the cloves with the flat side of a large knife, or roll in a garlic roller – the skin will easily peel away. Then sprinkle over a little salt and chop the garlic cloves. The garlic will mash easily once finely chopped, which is the best way to include it in dishes.

Cook's tip

Seafood is also an integral part of Spanish paellas, so try adding a few prawns, a little chopped fish or mussels about 10 minutes out from the end of cooking time.

Preparation Time: 10 minutes
Cooking Time: 15 minutes
Serves 4-6

*The critics, à la the crew,
offering their expert opinion.*

Cook's tip

If you have leftover stale
bread, crumb it up and freeze
in bags. Use for burgers,
crumbing foods, or for making
a savoury crumble; or for a
casserole, mornay or pie. Rub
50 grams of butter into 2 cups
of fresh breadcrumbs, ½ cup
grated cheese and sprinkle
over a pie and bake. It's easy
and delicious.

b b q burgers

Burgers are a prerequisite for the BBQ. The inclusion of finely chopped gherkins adds a fabulous flavour to the burger, and BBQ Sauce in place of tomato will give the burgers more of a kick. I like to serve my burgers with some lettuce, a few tomato slices on top, a little avocado and of course some Wattie's beetroot. . . Now where would a good Kiwi burger be without beetroot? Even McDonald's use it!

Ingredients

750 grams lean minced beef

1 egg

3 spring onions, trimmed and finely chopped

¼ cup chopped fresh parsley or 1 tblsp dried

about 4 large gherkins, finely chopped

¾ cup fresh wholemeal breadcrumbs

½ cup **Wattie's BBQ Sauce**

½ tsp each salt and pepper to season

1-2 tblsp oil (for pan-frying or BBQ)

Toppings

burger buns

tomato slices

lettuce

Wattie's sliced beetroot

avocado slices

Method

1 In a bowl combine the minced beef, egg, spring onions, parsley, gherkins, breadcrumbs and BBQ sauce and season with salt and pepper. Mix well.

2 Mould into 8 patties with a wet hand.

3 Pre-heat the BBQ or grill. BBQ or grill for about 5-7 minutes on each side until the burgers are well browned and cooked. If you plan to pan fry the burgers, then heat the oil in a frying pan and add the burgers, cooking over a moderately high heat for about the same time. Serve in buns with favourite toppings and maybe some potato wedges on the side.

c h i c k e n
stroganoff
on pasta

Stroganoff hails from Russia and is traditionally made with beef. In this version I've used chicken for a change but you could use about 400 grams of finely sliced beef rump. For a flavour burst add ¼ - ½ cup of finely sliced gherkins and a dash of brandy.

Ingredients

4 single **Tegel chicken breasts**, skin removed

a little oil for pan frying

2 onions, finely sliced

2 cups finely sliced mushrooms

¼ cup white wine, chicken stock or water

300 gram can **Wattie's Just Add Creamy Mushroom and Herb Chicken Simmer Sauce**

½ - ¾ cup sour cream

1 packet **Wattie's Fresh Fettuccine** or **Spaghetti pasta**

Method

1 Cut the fillet from the chicken underneath the breast and then slice all the chicken evenly into very thin slices. By removing the fillet, you make it easier and safer to slice.

2 Heat a good dash of oil in a frying pan.

3 Add the sliced onions and mushrooms and toss over a high heat for about 3-4 minutes, stirring regularly until they have browned and softened, but have not burnt.

4 Remove from the pan and add a touch more oil to the pan. Add the chicken in two batches and brown quickly over a high heat. You may find this better to do in batches rather than all at once, as the cold chicken can lower the pan temperature too much, and the chicken will stew as opposed to browning nicely.

5 Add the wine or stock or water to the pan and add the mushroom and onions with the simmer sauce.

6 Stir and then add the sour cream. Stir, cover and simmer over a moderate heat for about 12-15 minutes until the chicken is cooked.

7 Bring a large pot of water to the boil with 1 tblsp salt. Add the fresh pasta and cook according to the directions on the packet. Drain well and toss through the chicken sauce. Serve hot.

Preparation Time: 15 minutes
Cooking Time: 20 minutes
Serves 4-6

Propping the kitchen is always fun and most of what appears on the set comes from favourite shops and friends as well as a large personal collection. In particular I collect butter churns of all shapes and sizes. This Australian churn was located in the south of Tasmania one year while home on holidays and was carried carefully all the way back to New Zealand. The stewards on Air New Zealand thought me slightly mad, but it takes pride of place on the set each shoot and looks fabulous.

Preparation Time: 15-20 minutes
Cooking Time: 45 minutes
Serves 5-6

Cook's tip

Baking blind material can be
dried rice or beans. Once used,
cool and store for later use. It
can be used again and again
and again. You can also
purchase metal baking blind
beans; however I find dried
beans and rice just as good and
at next to no cost.

Warwick – my best friend and
husband, and the man who
keeps the wheels rolling when
all gets just too busy. He's
great – especially on dishes ar
keeping our cat 'Sooty' fed anc
happy too.

south of
the border *pie*

Pumpkin has an affinity with beans, especially these Spicy Mexican Beans, and mixed together, as they have been here, they make a wonderful pie. The pastry base is baked blind so that your pie has a buttery crisp shell.

Ingredients

2 sheets pre-rolled savoury pastry

1 tblsp oil

1 onion, finely chopped

2 stalks celery, trimmed and finely chopped

1 potato, washed and finely chopped

1 courgette, finely chopped

1 can **Craig's Spicy Mexican Beans**

2 tomatoes, chopped

handful chopped parsley

¼ can water

about 2 cups mashed pumpkin

sprinkling grated Cheddar cheese

Method

1 Roll the two sheets of pastry together and use to line the base and sides of a 24 cm flan tin, preferably metal.

2 Line the pastry with baking paper and pour in sufficient baking blind material to ½ fill the tin.

3 Bake at 200°C for 15 minutes. Remove the baking blind material (see Cook's Tip) and paper and return the base to the oven for a further 2 minutes.

4 Heat the oil in a frying pan and cook the onion, celery potato and courgette for 2-3 minutes. Add the Spicy Mexican Beans, tomatoes, parsley and water and simmer for 15 minutes until the potatoes are cooked.

5 Pile into the pastry lined flan tin.

6 Spread the mashed pumpkin on top and sprinkle with grated Cheddar cheese.

7 Bake at 220°C oven for 30-35 minutes until hot and golden. Serve hot.

summer
chicken

This is one of my favourite ways of serving chicken. You can use this method to cook a whole chicken also; just use a sharp pair of kitchen scissors and remove the backbone. Flatten the chicken and place the stuffing under the skin. Bake for 1¼-1½ hours. Vary the flavours with the honey you use – there are so many to choose from. Rewa Rewa, Manuka, Honeydew, Clover, Lavender . . . the choice is almost endless and each will bring its own unique flavour.

Ingredients

4 **Tegel leg and thigh portions**

¼ cup chopped fresh herbs (parsley, chives or thyme)

2 tblsp honey

grated rind one lemon

2 tblsp butter

pepper to season

Method

1 Carefully rub your thumb or finger between the skin and the meat on the leg and thigh portions to release the skin from the meat.

2 In a bowl mix together the chopped herbs, honey, lemon rind and butter and season well with pepper.

3 Place ¼ of this mixture under the skin of each chicken portion, pressing down firmly with the hand to ensure that the filling spreads out right along the chicken under the skin.

4 Place the chicken portions on a rack above a baking dish. Bake at 180°C for 50-60 minutes until the portions are well cooked. Depending on the size of the portions it may take the full 60 minutes. To test if cooked, pierce the meat with a skewer at the thickest part of the portion. The juice should be clear; if it's still pink return to the oven for a further 5 minutes and test again. Serve with a salad of summer vegetables and fruits, tossed in vinaigrette.

Cook's tip

To keep herbs, wash well in cold water and shake off excess water. Place in a plastic bag (freezer bag) and blow up with your own air. Twist the top together, seal the top with a twisty tie and keep in the refrigerator. Herbs keep well stored this way.

Add the grated rind of two oranges to a sweet scone mixture and serve scones with marmalade and cream.

Pare the rind from an orange and add to a lamb casserole, or mince with mint and chopped shallots and use to rub over a leg of lamb before roasting.

Grate the rind and squeeze the juice from a couple of limes and mix with 100 grams softened butter and use to dot over a slice of grilled fish.

Grate lemon rind over freshly steamed vegetables with a good seasoning of pepper and a squeeze of juice. Does wonders for courgettes and green beans.

Preparation Time: 10 minutes
Cooking Time: 15 minutes
Serves 4

Cook's tip

Baking and cooking paper are
the same thing, they are just
made by two different
companies. (A chemist's parcel
fold is where the two sides are
brought together and folded
over twice to seal. The ends
are then folded to a point and
tucked underneath.)

This photo sits on my desk at
home, so I thought I'd just sneak
in! From memory my Dad was
cooking scones for my Mum for
Mother's Day one year when they
visited. They're both octogenarian
now and, yes, they still both cook
— it must run in the family!

sweet chilli fish
in paper

One of the nicest ways to cook fish is to wrap it up in paper so that it cooks with all the juices inside the parcel. You'll need cooking or baking paper for this, not greaseproof. There are two ways of wrapping the fish – the one we demonstrated on Food in a Minute and another way described here, where you have less paper and the parcel puffs up beautifully. I prefer the second way, so do give it a go.

Ingredients

baking or cooking paper

4 x 150 gram firm white fish fillets (terakihi, orange roughy, John dory or snapper)

¼ cup each finely sliced courgettes and mushrooms

*½ can **Wattie's Sweet Chilli Stir Fry Sauce***

Method

1 Cut four large lengths of baking or cooking paper about 30-35 cm long.

2 In the middle of each piece place a fish fillet. Top with a quarter of the vegetables and about 3 tablespoonfuls of the chilli sauce.

3 Bring the sides together above the centre of the fish and fold the edges over each other like a chemist's parcel. Fold the ends to a point and tuck underneath the parcel. Place each parcel on a baking tray. Alternatively cut a large piece of baking or cooking paper about 30 cm long. Cut a large heart from the paper. Place fish and ingredients on one half of the heart. Fold the other half over and then pleat the edges together.

4 Bake at 200°C for 12-15 minutes. The timing will depend on the thickness of the fish. Medium size fillets will take 12 minutes. For thicker fillets allow the 15 minutes. Serve with potatoes and a few extra vegetables tossed in the remaining sweet chilli sauce.

t u s c a n
chicken

Chicken casseroles could not be easier, and this one, cooked in a lidded frying pan, takes less than 45 minutes from start to finish. You can add more Italian flavours, with a handful of chopped fresh herbs such as parsley and oregano and a few capers. For a real knockout, chop up one well drained can of anchovies and stir in.

Ingredients

8 **Tegel chicken drumsticks**

1 tblsp flour

2 tblsp oil

2 onions, peeled and sliced

about 2 cups mushrooms, halved

425 gram can **Wattie's Italian Seasoned Tomatoes**

12 stuffed green olives

plenty freshly ground black pepper

pasta for 4 to accompany (shape of your choice)

Wattie's Frozen Whole Baby Beans to accompany

Method

1   Remove the skin from the drumsticks if wished. It will help us trim excess fat from the meal. Put the flour into a bag and toss the chicken legs in the flour.

2   Heat the oil in a large lidded non-stick frying pan.

3   Add the chicken pieces and brown over a moderately high heat for 10 minutes, turning regularly so that the chicken browns evenly.

4   Add the onions, mushrooms, Italian tomatoes, olives and season well with freshly ground black pepper.

5   Cover and simmer over a low heat for 20 minutes.

6   Serve with the beans and hot, freshly cooked pasta tossed with a little butter and fresh herbs.

Preparation Time: 10 minutes
Cooking Time: 30 minutes
Serves 4

Parmesan cheese adds a wonderful flavour to any Italian flavoured meal.
Grated Parmesan cheese or other hard cheese can be stored in the freezer for
later use. Store in an airtight container.

Cook's tip

The fat on a chicken is mainly
attached to the skin which in
itself is also high in fat. By
removing the skin where
possible, like here in Tuscan
Chicken, we help keep the fat
count down.

Preparation Time: 10 minutes
Cooking Time: 30 minutes
Serves 4

Cook's tip

Herbs that would go well here
include majoram, oregano,
Italian or curly parsley, chives or
finely chopped rosemary. Make
garlic pizza bread by spreading
pizza bases with garlic butter
and a sprinkling of grated
Parmesan cheese. Grill or bake
until golden, garnish with
chopped parsley and cut into
wedges. Serve piping hot.

If a saucepan gets left on the stove and the
bottom gets burnt, pour in cold water with
2 teaspoons baking soda. Left to soak
overnight the pot comes clean easily with
steel wool.

meatballs

Everyone's always looking for a new way to serve mince. Herbed pork mince meatballs are cooked in a rich Mediterranean tomato sauce and served on top of fettuccine. If your an olive lover (sadly I'm not) hide a de-stoned black olive or stuffed green olive in the centre of each meatball before cooking. Top with a little grated Parmesan cheese and a fresh herb like parsley to serve, and add a crispy salad and some toasted pizza bread on the side. Why not serve with garlic pizza bread? See the Cook's Tip.

Ingredients

500 grams minced pork

½ cup chopped fresh herbs or 2 tblsp dried

1 onion, finely chopped

1 slice white bread, crumbed

1 egg

salt and pepper to season

2 tblsp oil or clarified butter

½ cup red wine or chicken stock or water

400 gram can **Wattie's Mediterranean Tomatoes**

1 packet **Wattie's Fresh Fettuccine Pasta**

Garnish: grated Parmesan cheese, fresh herbs (optional)

Method

1   In a bowl mix together the pork, herbs, onion, bread and egg. Season the mixture well with salt and pepper. Roll the mixture into 24 balls.

2   Heat the oil in a frying pan and cook the meatballs until they are evenly browned all over. Add the red wine and simmer 5 minutes.

3   Stir in the Mediterranean tomatoes. Cover and simmer for 20 minutes.

4   Cook the fresh fettuccine according to directions on the back of the packet. Drain well and toss in a little oil. Divide between four bowls and top with the meatballs.

5   Garnish with cheese and herbs.

roast turkey
with apple, lemon and walnut stuffing

Trying to do a perfect roast turkey in a minute, complete with stuffing and gravy was a daunting task for the cooks as well as the production team. Assistant Sarah-Jane started at dawn to have the perfect roast cooked early so we could say hello and goodbye before filming the rest of the cooking. All was going well until we had to show the removal of the giblets and neck, which was almost too much for the guys on the set who'd never seen how you prepare a turkey before. Once over that hurdle the filming moved on with turkey sandwiches for all, for days after. This first stuffing was prepared for our mid-winter Christmas Food in a Minute programme.

Ingredients

3.5 kg **Tegel turkey**

Stuffing

2 tblsp butter

2 rashers rindless bacon, diced

1 cup finely chopped onion

1 cup chopped parsley

1 apple, cored and finely chopped

70 gram packet chopped walnuts

grated rind one lemon

3 cups fresh white breadcrumbs

1 egg

pepper to season

Gravy

pan juices

4 tblsp flour

1 tblsp wholeseed mustard

2 tblsp lemon juice

1 cup chicken stock

Method

1 Defrost the turkey following the instruction on the packet. Do not underestimate the time required. Always defrost the turkey in the fridge, not on the bench, as this is a great way to catch bugs, even in winter.

2 Remove the giblets and neck and use these for making stock with 2 cups water and a stalk of celery and half an onion if you like. Wash the turkey cavity out well and wipe well with a paper towel.

3 Heat the butter in a frying pan and cook the bacon and onion for 5 minutes until the onion is softened. Remove from the heat and add the parsley, apple, walnuts, lemon rind, the breadcrumbs and egg. Stir together quickly, season with pepper and mix well.

4 Spoon the stuffing into the turkey cavity. Tie the turkey legs together with string or cotton. Tuck the wings underneath.

5 Place the turkey in a roasting bag and place into a baking dish.

6 Roast the turkey following the instructions on the back of the turkey packet.

7 When cooked remove the turkey from the pan and allow to stand for 20 minutes, while preparing the gravy.

8 Strain off any pan juices into a jug and allow the fat and juice to separate out. Return about 4 tblsp of the fat to the pan and discard the remaining fat.

9 Add the flour to the pan and cook over a low heat for 2-3 minutes until frothy. Measure the reserved pan juices and make up to 1½ cups with water or extra chicken stock. Stir into the pan with the mustard, lemon juice and chicken stock. Simmer until thickened and season with pepper if wished. Carve the turkey and serve with spoonfuls of stuffing, roast vegetables and the gravy.

Defrost Time: up to 2 days
Preparation Time: 30 minutes
Cooking Time: size dependent
– 2½ hours plus
Serves 6-10
This is sufficient stuffing for a
3.5 to 4.5 kg turkey

Variations

Ingredients

This stuffing appeared in our Christmas Food in a Minute programme and makes a good variation.

½ cup each Brazil, pecan, almond and macadamia nuts (or 2 cups in total of nuts of your choice)

3 chopped spring onions

1 cup finely chopped dried apricots

grated rind and diced flesh of one orange

2 cups fresh breadcrumbs

2 tblsp chopped fresh herbs

Method

Toast all the nuts in a 180°C oven for 10-12 minutes until the nuts are golden. Allow to cool and then chop roughly.

In a bowl mix together the nuts, spring onions, apricots, orange rind and flesh, breadcrumbs and herbs. Season well with pepper and salt.

Preparation Time: 15 minutes
Cooking Time: 15-20 minutes
Serves 4

Cook's tip

Add a little more flavour to boiled rice with spices and flavourings as it cooks. A cinnamon stick, bayleaf, blade of mace, diced onion, a few cloves or a piece of ginger will all bring flavour to rice. And don't forget the salt with rice; it's very bland without it.

If you want to jazz up Lamb Satay add a couple of sliced chillies. But beware – these little monsters can be fierier than you think! Their heat is caused by capsaicin, a potent chemical in chillies that survives freezing and processing. On top of causing a burning sensation in your mouth, chillies trigger the brain to produce endorphins, natural painkillers that promote a sense of well-being and stimulation.

In general the smaller the chilli the hotter it is; this is because the smaller chillies have larger amounts of seeds and veins relative to their overall size and these are the parts that contain up to 80 pert cent of the capsaicin in the chilli.

You can remove these parts but remember to wear rubber gloves as it is all too easy to rub an eye with some of the capsaicin still on your hands or under nails and this can cause burning. Always wash hands well after preparing fresh chillies.

summer
lamb satay
with noodles

Lamb steaks are a versatile cut of meat and here I used them to make a satay stir fry. Finely diced, stir fried, with seasonal vegetables and cooked in Wattie's Satay Stir Fry Sauce, it was another very popular idea.

Ingredients

500 grams lamb steaks (2 large or 4 small steaks)

1 tblsp oil

1 onion, peeled and finely sliced

3 cups sliced green summer vegetables (asparagus, beans, courgettes, peppers etc.)

425 gram can **Wattie's Satay Stir Fry Sauce**

1 cup crispy fried noodles

handful of roasted peanuts to garnish (optional)

Method

1   Trim any fat from the lamb steaks and then cut the meat into very small 1 cm pieces.

2   Heat the oil in a frying pan until very hot and add the meat. Toss quickly over the hot heat to brown and seal the lamb. Do this in two batches to ensure that the lamb does not stew.

3   Add the onion and cook for one minute. Add all the summer vegetables and toss for 1-2 minutes.

4   Stir in the satay sauce and cover. Simmer 4-5 minutes.

5   Toss the crispy fried noodles though the sauce before serving. Garnish with peanuts if wished. Serve on a large platter with plenty of boiled rice.

fettuccine *pasta*

with peas and parmesan

When I presented this dish on the set to be cooked, the crew thought it would be awfully dull with peas in it, but the finished product changed their minds. Peas are crunchy and sweet, and go very well with bacon and Parmesan. It's a simple dish, but one that's delicious.

Ingredients

4 rashers bacon, trimmed of rind

2 tblsp oil

1 onion, finely chopped

½ cup chicken stock

½ cup cream

*1 cup **Wattie's Baby Garden Peas***

1 tblsp salt

*400 gram packet **Wattie's Fresh Egg Fettuccine Pasta***

½ cup grated Parmesan or tasty Cheddar cheese

Method

1 Finely slice or dice the bacon. Heat the oil in a frying pan and add the onion and bacon. Cook over a moderate heat for about 5 minutes, stirring frequently until the onion and bacon are soft and lightly coloured but not burnt.

2 Add the chicken stock, cream and peas, and simmer ever so gently for about 5 minutes while cooking the pasta.

3 Have a large saucepan full of boiling water and add the salt. Add the fresh fettuccine pasta and stir well with a spoon or fork to separate the pasta strips. Boil rapidly for 4-5 minutes until the pasta is cooked — no longer or you will overcook fresh pasta. Drain well and return to the saucepan.

4 Pour over the hot sauce and sprinkle over the Parmesan or Cheddar cheese. Ladle quickly into pasta bowls to serve. Serve with crusty bread and a tomato salad if wished.

Old crocks are another favourite item I collect. We never seem to travel anywhere without a new one finding its way home to adorn the set. The best ones seem to be found in Christchurch and around the South Island. I love scouring the old shops for them, it's a fabulous past-time and a great way to meet people.

Preparation Time: 5 minutes
Cooking Time: 10 minutes
Serves 4

Cook's tip

Tightly seal open bags of frozen food that are being returned to the freezer, as it's easy for air to get in and cause freezer burn on your food.

Preparation Time: 15 minutes
Cooking Time: 12-15 minutes
Serves 4-5

Cook's tip

Soy sauce comes in many
varieties but there are two main
Chinese versions, light and dark.
The dark soy sauce is more
pungent and best used for
marinades and the light soy
sauce for shaking on top of your
food before enjoying. If you
prefer, change the peanuts to
cashews for a real flavour burst.

If it all looks glamorous,
then believe me, at times it
not. Here I work to reprodu
the food for stills
photography. By this time I
have tested or cooked the
recipes four times and the
taste-buds are beginning to
wish for something new.

sweet & sour
chicken
with honey roasted peanuts

Every so often we have Asian food in our home so as to enjoy the flavour of ginger, garlic, chilli, honey – all served up on perfect steamed rice. With this recipe you can vary the final flavour by using different seasonal vegetables.

Ingredients

about 1 tblsp each runny honey and soy sauce

4 **Tegel chicken thigh and leg portions**

dash oil

3 cups chopped vegetables of your choice (I like to have broccoli, leeks, onions, celery, carrots)

227 gram can pineapple chunks in juice

300 gram can **Wattie's Just Add Sweet and Sour Chicken Simmer Sauce**

½-1 cup honey roasted peanuts (available from the supermarket)

Method

1 Mix the soy sauce and honey together in a large bowl or dish.

2 Pull the chicken skin from the chicken portions and cut the meat from the bones. Then cut into dice. The meat off the thighs and legs has more flavour for something like this dish and is much more economical. You can use breast meat if you prefer. Toss in the honey and soy sauce and leave to marinate for about 10 minutes.

3 Heat the oil in a frying pan and brown the chicken pieces over a high heat for about 5 minutes so they are nicely browned and half cooked. Transfer to a plate.

4 Add the vegetables to the hot pan and toss for 2 minutes. Add the pineapple and juice, and the simmer sauce. Stir and return the chicken to the pan.

5 Stir over heat for 5-7 minutes until the chicken and vegetables are all cooked.

6 Toss in the peanuts just before serving. Serve over freshly cooked boiled rice.

french beef
& mushroom cottage pie

My first challenge with Potato Pom Poms was also Food in a Minute's greatest ever success. Using them to top a cottage pie in place of having to cook and mash potatoes seemed to register with all the viewers and sales increased so much that, many supermarkets ran out of stock.

Ingredients

1 tblsp oil

1 onion, finely chopped

500 grams minced beef

135 gram can **Wattie's Tomato Paste**

560 gram can **Wattie's Just Add Country French Mince Simmer Sauce**

2 cups chopped mushrooms

about 1 cup **Wattie's frozen Peas and Corn**

1 cup or half a can of water

400 gram packet **Wattie's Golden Heart Potato Pom Poms**

$^1/_2$ cup grated tasty Cheddar cheese

Method

1   Heat the oil in a frying pan and brown the onion and minced beef, breaking up the beef with a fork as you go to ensure even sized pieces.

2   Add the tomato paste and cook, stirring over a moderate heat until it has darkened in colour to a deeper brown shade. This takes about 5 minutes and adds a wonderful rich flavour to the pie.

3   Add the simmer sauce, mushrooms, peas and corn, and water.

4   Stir, cover and simmer for 15 minutes. Stir occasionally.

5   Transfer to a 6-cup capacity oven-proof dish, top with pom poms and sprinkle over the grated Cheddar cheese.

6   Bake at 220°C for about 15-20 minutes until the topping is golden, the cheese bubbling and the pie hot and delicious.

Copper adds warmth to the set and these three items, a pre-electric Fowlers Vacola bottling unit, an Indian samovar and French copper saucepans are always dotted on the set.

Preparation Time: 20 minutes
Cooking Time: 40 minutes
Serves 4-5

Cook's tip

Browning tomato paste for casseroles, soups or pies is a great trick to remember. It adds a real depth of flavour and more intense colour to your sauce. Stir the tomato paste all the time over a moderate heat so it browns rather than burns. It also acts as a thickener, eliminating the need to add extra flour.

Preparation Time: 10 minutes
Marinating Time: 1 hour
or overnight
Cooking Time: 15 minutes
Serves 4

Cook's tip

Meat marinated with sugars
like honey needs to be
cooked gently otherwise the
sugar will burn before the
meat is cooked.

*Flowers always play a large part in the studio set and
there are favourites. For me it's sunflowers with their
bright petals and rich centres. We're always trying to
match up the flowers with the colours in the food or
place-setting each time. With any luck, at the end of
the shoot Anna and I get to take them home.*

citrus
honey chicken
with chunky peach sauce

In our house summer's the one time I manage to get a break from cooking. It's when Warwick takes to the BBQ – for better or worse! I've learnt to hide the BBQ fork so that only tongs are used; this way the meat will not be punctured and turned into a sieve – and will remain moist! Adding a fruit sauce jazzes up even the most basic BBQ cuisine.

Ingredients

2 tblsp oil (olive is preferable)

grated rind and juice of one orange

2 tblsp liquid honey

1 tblsp chopped rosemary leaves

4 **single breasts of Tegel chicken**, skin removed

Chunky Peach Sauce

410 gram can **Wattie's Peach Slices in Juice**

1 spring onion, trimmed and finely chopped

2 tsp grated fresh ginger

½ chilli or dash of chilli pepper

1 tblsp white wine vinegar

Method

Chicken

1 Mix together the oil, orange rind and juice, honey and rosemary leaves. Place the chicken in a non-metallic dish and pour over the marinade. Leave covered in the refrigerator for 1 hour or overnight. The longer you leave the marinade the more intense the flavour.

2 Heat a little extra oil or butter in a non-stick frying pan and cook the chicken over a moderate heat for 4-5 minutes each side until the chicken is golden and cooked. Alternatively, grill or BBQ the chicken under a high heat for 5-6 minutes each side. Brush with the marinade while cooking. Serve the chicken with the Chunky Peach Sauce.

Chunky Peach Sauce

1 Place the well-drained peach slices into a food processor. Add the spring onion, grated ginger, chilli powder and white wine vinegar and pulse until well chopped but not too smooth.

m u s h r o o m
lasagne

When we decided to prepare lasagne for Food in a Minute we all agreed that it was essential to show how to prepare a proper cheese sauce, which is so important in the final flavour. As a result, as we tried to fit everything into our one-minute slot, the layering of the lasange looked like it was on 'fast-forward'!

Ingredients

Cheese Sauce

50 grams butter

3 tblsp flour

1½ cups milk

1½ cups grated Cheddar or similar cheese

pepper to season (optional)

Meat Filling

1 onion, peeled and chopped

500 grams minced beef, pork or chicken

2 tblsp oil

1 can **Wattie's Traditional Pasta Sauce**

2 cups finely sliced mushrooms

½ can water

½ x 250 gram box San Remo lasagne sheets

Method

Cheese Sauce

1 Heat the butter in a saucepan and add the flour. Cook for one minute until frothy. Add the milk and stir over a moderate heat for 2-3 minutes until thick and glossy. Stir in one cup of the grated cheese, remove from the heat and season with pepper if wished.

Meat Filling

1 Heat the oil in a frying pan. Add the onion and beef and brown well over a high heat, breaking up the mince as you go.

2 Add the can of pasta sauce, water and sliced mushrooms and stir well. Cover and simmer for 10 minutes.

To assemble

1 Grease the inside of a 6-cup capacity oven-proof dish. Place a layer of pasta sheets on the base of the dish. Spread over half the meat sauce and then top with one third of the cheese sauce.

2 Repeat the layers finishing with a layer of pasta and cheese sauce. Sprinkle over the remaining ½ cup cheese.

3 Bake at 190°C for 30 minutes until hot and golden.

Preparation Time: 20 minutes
Cooking Time: 30 minutes
Serves 6

66

fruity devilled *sausages*

For the programme on this dish I ordered the sausages to be specially made by our local butcher 'The Meat Keeper' so that there would be no way the skins would split during the filming of them cooking. While collecting them I inquired also whether they should be pierced before cooking and was told that unless you cook them in too hot a pan, sausages won't split. The practice is a hangover from the war years when flour was used instead of breadcrumbs as a filler and the sausages expanded far more, causing them to split!

Ingredients

1 tblsp oil

8 really tasty, thick beef or pork sausages

1 apple, cored and sliced

1 onion, peeled and sliced

½ cup sultanas

227 gram can of pineapple pieces and juice

560 gram can **Wattie's Just Add Devilled Sausage Simmer Sauce**

Method

1 Heat the oil in a frying pan and add the sausages. Brown on both sides over a low heat so they do not split their skins.

2 Add the apple, onion, sultanas, pineapple and juice and can of simmer sauce.

3 Stir, cover and simmer over a low heat for 30 minutes.

4 Serve the sausages with plenty of hearty mashed potato and vegetables.

Preparation Time: 5 minutes
Cooking Time: 30-35 minutes
Serves 4

Cook's tip

In place of pineapple, use a well-drained can of **Wattie's Peach Slices** — you'll find they will go well with the **Wattie's Devilled Simmer Sauce**.

Preparation Time: 15-20 minutes
Cooking Time: 1¼ hours
Serves 4-6

Cook's tip

Adding a couple of rashers of
bacon and 200 grams of
mushrooms will create a
fabulous variation. Seasoned
flour is made by adding salt
and pepper to plain flour. A
good grinding of both
seasonings added to ½ cup of
flour is about right.

*Always store fresh meat in the refrigerator. It
should be kept as dry as possible and shouldn't
sit in its own drip or moisture. Cold air must be
able to circulate freely around the meat in the
fridge and meat must not be placed beside warm
items at any time. Meat should be used within
two days or purchase. Leave in its original
packing in the coldest part of the fridge.*

hearty beef casserole

with beer

Casseroles are an easy option for winter meals as once the preparation is done they simmer along under their own steam until cooked. This beef casserole is a variation on Belgium's Beef Carbonnade which is made with very dark ale. The ale adds mellow nuttiness. You can add whatever type of beer you like – though I'd refrain from using stout. The other important ingredient is the minestrone soup which has plenty of flavour and a great selection of ingredients to add body and texture.

Ingredients

650 - 750 grams blade or chuck steak, trimmed of fat

¼ cup seasoned flour

2 tblsp oil

355 ml can beer

1 onion, peeled and roughly chopped

1 large carrot, peeled and roughly chopped

2 stalks celery, trimmed and chopped

1 large parsnip, peeled and roughly chopped

*560 gram can **Wattie's Hearty Minestrone Soup** or 2 X 300 gram cans **Wattie's Minestrone Soup for One***

Method

1 Cut the meat into large 3 cm pieces and toss in the seasoned flour.

2 Heat the oil in a large lidded frying pan and brown the meat pieces on all sides. Browning will add colour and flavour to the finished casserole.

3 Add the beer and simmer quickly, uncovered, for 5 minutes. You need to reduce the beer by a quarter.

4 Add the onion, carrot, celery, parsnip and minestrone soup and bring to a simmer. Cover and simmer gently for 1¼ hours until tender. Alternatively, transfer to a casserole and cook at 180°C.

5 Serve with mashed potatoes and vegetables

butter chicken

Warwick and I are fans of Indian food and our love for this cuisine took us on a trip to Southern India to retrace the spice trail and sample the food first-hand. India is a country where all your senses seem real and alive. There's so much to see and do. One of our favourite dishes is Butter Chicken, which is tandoori chicken in a smooth creamy tomato sauce. With Wattie's Indian Spiced Tomatoes now available, this dish can be easily made at home now.

Ingredients

6 **Tegel Chicken leg and thigh portions**

1 medium onion, peeled and quartered

1 cup natural unsweetened yoghurt

1 tsp each ground ginger and garam masala

¼ tsp chilli powder

2 cans **Wattie's Indian Spiced Tomatoes**

½ cup cream

an oversized knob of butter (about 50 grams)

2 tblsp chopped coriander (optional)

Method

1 Cut the chicken portions in half and then remove the skin. Slash each portion deeply in three places. Place in one layer in a non-metallic dish.

2 In a food processor, process the onion, yoghurt and spices. Pour over the chicken and turn to coat evenly. Cover and refrigerate for at least one hour or up to 8 hours. (The longer you can leave the chicken to marinate, the more intense the flavour will be.)

3 Remove the chicken from the marinade, brush off any excess. Bake on a grill tray at 230°C for 20-25 minutes until well browned and cooked.

4 While the chicken is cooking prepare the sauce. Simmer the two cans of Indian tomatoes in a saucepan until reduced by half. Stir in the cream, butter and coriander and keep warm. Do not boil, or the sauce will curdle.

5 Serve the chicken coated in the butter sauce. Serve with rice, poppadums, chutneys, fresh bananas – sliced, tossed in lemon juice and desiccated coconut.

The spice markets of India.

Preparation Time: 15 minutes
Marinating Time: 1-8 hours
Cooking Time: 20-30 minutes
Serves 4-6

Cook's tip

Tandoori and Butter Chicken are usually deep crimson red. If you would like to achieve this look, mix together 2 tblsp yellow and 1 tblsp red food colouring. Once you have slashed the chicken brush it well with the colouring and continue from Step 2.

Preparation Time: 15 minutes
Cooking Time: 15-20 minutes
Serves 4

The final shot gets just a glaze of pan juices before shooting. I insist that there is no cheating with our food photography. What you see is exactly what you will get.

Cook's tip

Chicken breasts seem to vary in size when you buy them, sometimes with or without the tenderloin fillet. This recipe was tested without the tenderloin fillet. Puff pastry needs a hot oven in which to rise and cook properly, so place these pies to the top of a well-heated oven. A more golden glaze for pastry can be achieved by using beaten egg for the glaze in place of milk.

c h i c k e n &
spinach pies

These Chicken Pies are ideal to have hot in winter or cold on picnics. If you serve t
he pies hot, when your family opens them up they'll be greeted with wonderful aro
mas. And it's important not to forget the nutmeg, as this magical spice is the best
partner to spinach you'll ever find.

Ingredients

4 boneless **Tegel chicken breasts**,
skin removed

250 gram packet **Wattie's Frozen
Chopped Spinach**, defrosted

3 tblsp cream cheese

¼ tsp each nutmeg, salt and white
pepper

2 sheets frozen pre-rolled puff
pasty, defrosted

milk to glaze

Method

1 Remove the skin from the chicken breasts.

2 Squeeze the spinach between two plates to remove all
   the excess moisture. The spinach needs to be really
   dry to ensure that you do not end up with soggy
   pastry when the pies cook.

3 Mix the spinach with the cream cheese, nutmeg, salt
   and pepper.

4 Take the pastry sheets and cut in half diagonally. Place
   a quarter of the spinach mixture in the centre of each
   triangle and place the chicken breast on top.

5 Bring the long ends down to cover the chicken and
   fold the thicker corner on top to completely enclose.
   Pinch ends together.

6 Transfer to a greased baking tray. Brush with milk to
   glaze.

7 Bake at 220°C for 15-20 minutes until hot and golden.

creamy tomato fettuccine

Pasta meals are so often the ideal option for busy people and there are so many variations to a theme you could go on forever. This recipe could easily include meat, chicken or fish in place of bacon. Just finely slice about 200 grams of your preference and add in place of the bacon. Alternatively leave the bacon out and make it a vegetarian meal.

Ingredients

4-6 rashers bacon, trimmed of rind

2 tblsp oil

250 grams mushrooms, finely sliced

½ cup white wine

425 gram can **Wattie's Tomato and Herb Pasta Sauce**

¼ cup cream

¼ cup chopped fresh parsley

fettuccine for 4

Parmesan cheese and fresh herbs to garnish

Method

1 Chop the bacon finely.

2 Heat the oil in a frying pan and add the bacon and mushrooms and cook over a moderately hot heat for 2 minutes until the bacon is fragrant and the mushrooms softened.

3 Add the wine and simmer until reduced by half.

4 Stir in the pasta sauce and simmer uncovered for 5 minutes.

5 Stir in the cream and chopped parsley and warm through. Do not boil or the sauce will curdle.

6 Cook the fettuccine in plenty of boiling salted water until 'al dente' (fresh 4-5 minutes, dried 11-12 minutes) and drain well. Serve in pasta bowls topped with the sauce and garnished with a little grated Parmesan cheese and herbs if wished.

All the props have to be selected the week before we shoot. They are all set out on large tables at the back of the studio for me to choose from. In addition there's a large number of cutlery sets, glassware and all those little things that go into making a setting. These change each time to keep up with the latest trends, making Anna's job rather nightmarish!

Preparation Time: 5-10 minutes
Cooking Time: 15 minutes
Serves 4

Cook's tip

Authentic Parmesan cheese comes from Italy and is easily distinguishable by it's price! It is however worth ever cent. Parmesan has a slightly granular texture and a nutty smoothness. It's best purchased by the piece and grated as required. A little goes a long way, making it cost effective.

Preparation Time: 20 minutes
Cooking Time: 1½ hours
Serves 4

Wattie's Tomato Sauce is probably our national condiment. While it's normally just squirted on at the last minute, there's plenty this humble sauce can do. Try one of these ideas.

- Mix 2 tablespoons with 1 cup mayonnaise with a good squirt of lemon juice, a dash of chilli powder and, if you wish, some horseradish sauce or horseradish mustard. Now you have a super cocktail mayonnaise to top a pasta and seafood salad.

- Pan-fry a beef steak and set aside. To the pan add a couple of tablespoons tomato sauce, a dash of Worcestershire sauce, a dollop of mustard and a good splash of red wine. Simmer and you have a steak Dianne sauce. Great with beef-burgers too.

Cook's tip

Casseroles always seem to have a more mellow flavour the next day, so preparing them a day or two in advance will only serve to improve the flavour.

winter
beef casserole

There are so many variations possible with this basic casserole recipe you could use lamb or chicken here instead of beef (use chicken stock as well). Vary the vegetables, add leeks in place of onions, pumpkin for carrots and try meaty flat mushrooms for a real flavour burst. My mother always liked to have pastry squares to garnish her casseroles. For these, cut a sheet of pre-rolled pastry into 16 even squares, glaze with milk and bake at 230°C for 10-12 minutes. These keep well in an airtight container.

Ingredients

750 grams cross-cut beef

2 tblsp seasoned flour

2-3 tblsp oil

½ cup **Wattie's Tomato Sauce**

2 tblsp Worcestershire sauce

1½ cups beef stock

2 onions, peeled and roughly cut

2 stalks celery, trimmed and chopped

1 carrot, peeled and diced

250 grams mushrooms, halved

chopped parsley to serve

Method

1 Trim the meat of any extra fat and cut into large 3 cm pieces.

2 Toss the meat in the seasoned flour.

3 Heat the oil in a frying pan and cook the meat over a high heat until it is well browned on all sides. Transfer to a casserole. Blend together the remaining seasoned flour with the tomato sauce, Worcestershire sauce and beef stock. Pour into the pan and bring to the boil. Transfer to the casserole.

4 Add the onions, celery, carrots and mushrooms to the pan and cook 3-4 minutes.

5 Cook on top of the stove for 1¼ - 1½ hours or in a 180°C oven for the same time. Season with pepper and chopped parsley and serve with plenty of mashed potatoes and Brussels sprouts or your favourite green vegetable.

herbed
porcupines

Mince is wonderfully versatile but so often we end up relying upon a small repertoire of well known ideas. These meatballs will be a favourite with everyone. The inclusion of rice in the meatballs means that as they gently cook the rice expands and sticks out of the meatballs, giving them a fabulous appearance and adding a super texture.

Ingredients

500 grams lean minced beef

½ cup uncooked long grain rice

¼ cup chopped fresh herbs, like thyme or parsley

salt and pepper to season

1 tblsp oil

1 onion, peeled and finely sliced

560 gram can **Wattie's Just Add Hearty Savoury Mince Simmer Sauce**

1½ cups water

Method

1 In a bowl mix together the minced beef, rice, herbs and season with salt and pepper.

2 Roll into 12-14 even shaped balls.

3 Heat the oil in a frying pan and add the onion. Cook 3-4 minutes until just wilted. Add the simmer sauce and water and bring to the boil.

4 Add the meatballs and cover. Simmer gently for 30 minutes, turning once during the cooking time. Serve with seasonal vegetables.

Preparation Time: 10 minutes
Cooking Time: 30 minutes
Serves 4-6

Cook's tip

You could use other **Wattie's Just Add Simmer Sauces** to vary the flavour of the Herbed Porcupines.
Try **Country French Mince** or **Savoury Mexican Mince**.

burritos

The simplicity of Mexican foods has always appealed to me. When friends or family get together and have to mix and match their own fillings like in these burritos, the conversation really gets going.

Ingredients

2 tblsp oil

500 grams minced beef

1 onion, peeled and finely chopped

2 cloves garlic, crushed, peeled and mashed to a paste

½ tsp each ground cumin and cinnamon

1 apple, cored and finely diced

½ cup raisins

*400 gram can **Wattie's Mexican Spiced Tomatoes***

pepper to season

70 gram packet (½ cup) flaked almonds, toasted (optional)

1 packet tortillas

To serve: tomato slices, avocado, cheese, lettuce, sour cream, sliced peppers

Method

1 Heat the oil in a frying pan and brown the minced beef and onion until the meat and onion are well browned.

2 Add the garlic, spices, apple and raisins and cook for 3 minutes.

3 Stir in the Mexican tomatoes and season with pepper. Cover and simmer over a low heat for 15 minutes. Stir in the flaked almonds if using. Serve the filling in tortillas wrapped up with a dollop of sour cream and prepared salad ingredients.

Preparation Time: 10 minutes
Cooking Time: 25 minutes
Serves 4-6

Cook's tip

Tortillas are sold in packs in the supermarket. You'll find them with the other Mexican ingredients. Burritos are flour tortillas rolled up to enclose a filling.

79

pacific sausages

The humble sausage has come a long way since I was a kid and the choice was beef or pork, thick or thin. Mixing today's sausage flavours like Mexican Pedro chilli, pineapple and pork, parsley and pork, curry supreme or even garlic, with one of Wattie's Just Add Simmer Sauces you can prepare an enormous variety of casseroles. Change the vegetables or fruit to add new flavours.

Ingredients

6-8 thick pork sausages

2 carrots, peeled and roughly chopped

1 green pepper, cored and deseeded or, 2 stalks celery, trimmed and roughly chopped

1 onion, peeled and roughly chopped

560 gram can **Wattie's Just Add Devilled Sausage Simmer Sauce**

227 gram can pineapple slices in juice, halved

Method

1 Brown the sausages in a non-stick lidded frying pan until they are well browned on both sides.

2 Add the carrots, pepper or celery, onion, simmer sauce and pineapple slices with juice. Cover and simmer gently over a moderate heat for 20 minutes.

3 Serve with rice, mashed kumara or potatoes and green vegetables.

Preparation Time: 10 minutes
Cooking Time: 30 minutes
Serves 4-6

desserts

apple muffins
with spicy topping

I like muffins best when they're hot from the oven served with plenty of butter, but then I'm a butter fan. This recipe makes the most tender apple muffins with a lovely spicy topping. You can imagine how fast these went on the set; they didn't even get time to cool. I had many calls regarding the quantity of baking powder in the recipe, the 2 tblsp is correct, as it is equivalent to 2 tsp per cup of flour (there are 3 teaspoons to a tablespoon).

Ingredients

3 cups flour

2 tblsp baking powder

¾ cup caster sugar

1 tsp each ground ginger and mixed spice

2 eggs

*400 gram can **Wattie's Simply Apple***

1½ cups milk

few drops vanilla essence

100 grams melted butter, cooled

16 walnut halves (optional)

Topping

Juice of one lemon

1 tsp each caster sugar and mixed spice, mixed together

Method

1 Sift the flour, baking powder, caster sugar and spices into a bowl.

2 Mix together the eggs, apple, milk and vanilla essence. Make a well in the centre of the bowl and pour in the apple and milk mixture. Stir gently with a holed spoon until the batter is just mixed. Fold through the butter.

3 Do not over-mix the batter mixture as the muffins will peak like Mt Everest. Lift the mixture up with the spoon and turn it over on top of the remaining mix in the bowl. Give the bowl a quarter turn and then repeat this lifting and mixing routine until all ingredients are just blended.

4 Three-quarters fill 16 well-greased muffin tins. Decorate each muffin with a walnut half, if using.

5 Bake at 220°C for about 15-20 minutes until well-risen, golden and cooked.

6 Remove from the oven and wait 2-3 minutes. Mix together the sugar and mixed spice for the topping. Brush the tops of the muffins with the lemon juice. Sprinkle over the mixed spice sugar.

cheese & corn muffins

To make savoury muffins, omit the spices, sugar and apple. Add 1 cup **Wattie's Mexi-corn**, ½ cup grated cheese and season with ½ tsp ground pepper.

Cook's tip

I always grease my muffin tins, even when they're non-stick. It's a precaution that will also ensure the longevity of the tins.

Preparation Time: 2 hours
Freezing Time: 6 hours
Serves 8-10

Mike and I look over some of the products that we have chosen to begin Allyson's Collections with. All the products have been sourced from New Zealand producers or suppliers and all are used on the set or in my home.

Cook's tip

You can add more flavours to the filling by including grated orange rind, lemon rind, a cup of dried mixed fruits, or even some white chocolate chips as well.

vanilla &
boysenberry
icecream cake

This icecream cake proved to be a huge success. The centre filling is made of whipped cream and fruit and is much firmer than the icecream, so cut the dessert with a hot knife.

Ingredients

2 litres **Tip Top Vanilla Icecream**

300 ml bottle cream

¼ cup icing sugar

430 gram can **Wattie's Boysenberries in Syrup**, well drained

½ cup chocolate chips

2 tblsp cocoa for dusting

Method

1 Spread half the icecream into the base of a 23 cm loose bottom cake tin. Place in the freezer. Place the remaining icecream back into the freezer.

2 Whip the cream and icing sugar together until very thick. Fold in the boysenberries and chocolate chips.

3 Spread the boysenberry cream over the base of the icecream in the cake tin. Return to the freezer for two hours.

4 Spread the remaining icecream over the boysenberry cream and return to the freezer for at least six hours and preferably overnight.

5 To serve, warm a cloth and run around the outside of the cake tin. Remove the sides of the cake tin and place the icecream cake onto a serving plate. Dust with cocoa and cut into wedges to serve.

peach & banana upside-down tart

Upside-down tarts make very easy desserts. When this Food in a Minute programme aired it was a huge success. I've used two bananas here, but that's purely a personal preference. You can add any number of variations, like apricots and bananas with ginger, or pear quarters with cardamom, or try Wattie's Simply Apple with chopped and dried apricots and orange rind.

Ingredients

25 grams butter

1 tsp mixed spice

2 tblsp brown sugar

410 gram can **Wattie's Peach Slices**, well drained

1-2 large bananas, sliced

1 pre-rolled sheet short butter pastry

whipped cream to accompany

Method

1   Mix the butter, mixed spice and brown sugar together and work until the mixture is lightly creamed.

2   Spread it over the base of a 23 cm loose bottom cake tin, leaving a 1 cm edge border free of the butter mixture. This is to ensure the pastry has somewhere to stick to hold the juices in from leaking out onto the oven floor.

3   Arrange the peach slices and banana slices on top. They can be scattered or arranged neatly — it's up to you.

4   Trim the edges of the pastry square to make it more round.

5   Arrange the pastry on top and tuck the edges down the side and press firmly onto the sides of the base of the cake tin.

6   Bake at 220°C for 15 minutes or until the pastry is golden and well cooked. Allow to stand for 5 minutes, before turning upside-down onto a serving platter. Serve hot with whipped cream.

Blue and lemon feature predominantly on the set. I love the freshness of lemon colours and the calmness of blue. Together they make the set a fabulous place to work in and so often the props we use just reinforce this.

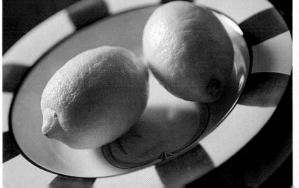

Preparation Time: 10 minutes
Cooking Time: 15-20 minutes
Serves 4-6

Cook's tip

It's important to allow this dish to stand for 5 minutes as the melted sugar underneath is extremely hot, so a little cooling time is a good idea.

Preparation Time: 15 minutes
Cooking Time: 40 minutes
Serves 6-8

Cook's tip

For a Coconut and Apple Tart,
remove ½ cup of the flour and
replace with ½ cup dessicated
coconut.

Fresh apples need to be kept in vented bags in the refrigerator. Make sure
they're somewhere away from being knocked as they will bruise easily.
Canned apple is a great product as it contains freshly diced apples tossed
in lemon juice, canned, sealed and cooked. It makes preparing a dessert
like the No Fuss Apple Tart a piece of cake — literally.

no fuss
apple tart

Desserts still seem to be popular with everyone, and we were delighted with the rave reviews from viewers and 'Next' readers to this Apple Tart. Jazz it up with some fresh passionfruit pulp mixed with the apple, or fold through a tablespoon or two of lemon honey for a change.

Ingredients

250 grams very soft butter (but not melted)

¾ cup caster sugar

1 egg

grated rind of 1 orange

1 tsp vanilla essence

2½ cups flour

2½ tsp baking powder

400 gram can **Wattie's Simply Apple**

icing sugar to serve with

(Note: If you don't have flour and baking powder, use 2½ cups self-raising flour.)

Method

1   In a bowl or food processor beat together the butter, caster sugar, egg, orange rind and vanilla essence until creamy and well mixed.

2   Add the flour and baking powder and stir or pulse to mix well.

3   Spread two-thirds of the mixture into the base of a well greased and floured 23 cm loose bottom cake tin.

4   Spread over the apple.

5   With floured hands dot the remaining dough over the top.

6   Bake at 190°C for 40 minutes. When cool dust with icing sugar and serve with lashings of whipped cream.

p e a c h &
yoghurt
m u f f i n s

The popularity of muffins is enormous, and there seems to be so many variations on a theme. These muffins have a fresh flavour from the use of yoghurt and cardamom. I like to serve them hot with plenty of butter melting into them.

Ingredients

¾ cup caster sugar

3 cups flour

1 tsp baking powder

1 tsp baking soda

1 tsp ground cardamom (or use ground ginger)

2 eggs

1 cup peach yoghurt

410 gram can **Wattie's Peach Slices in Clear Fruit Juice**

100 grams melted butter, cooled

Method

1 Sift the caster sugar, flour, baking powder, baking soda and ground cardamom or ginger into a large bowl.

2 In a blender or food processor mix together the eggs, yoghurt and peach slices with the juice.

3 Make a well in the centre of the dry ingredients and pour in the yoghurt mixture. Fold together with a holed spoon, folding in the melted butter as you go.

4 Divide between 12-16 well-greased muffin tins.

5 Bake at 220°C for 15-20 minutes until hot and golden.

Preparation Time: 10 minutes
Cooking Time: 20 minutes
Makes 12-16

Cook's tip

Use caster sugar for baking to achieve a finer texture. If you plan to freeze any muffins, freeze them while they are fresh and defrost them in the microwave or warm through in the oven.

queen rice
p u d d i n g

When I was a child my mother always had a pudding made for my brother and me every night. Versions on baked custard were always on the cards. Queen Pudding with its raspberry jam layer and fluffy meringue topping was always popular.

Ingredients

425 gram can **Wattie's Creamed Rice**, *vanilla flavoured*

1 cup milk

2 eggs

2 egg yolks

¼ cup caster sugar

4 tblsp **Craig's Raspberry Jam**

2 egg whites

Method

1 With a fork, mix together the creamed rice, milk, whole eggs, egg yolks and half the sugar. Pour into 4 well-greased 1 cup capacity sturdy tea cups or ramekins.

2 Place the cups in a large baking dish and take to the oven. Fill the baking dish with sufficient water to come one-third of the way up the sides of the cups. Bake at 180°C for 25-30 minutes until the custard has set in the cups or ramekins.

3 Carefully remove from the oven. Spread each cup with one tablespoonful of jam.

4 In a clean bowl beat the egg whites until stiff peaks form and then beat in the remaining sugar until the mixture is fluffy and meringue like.

5 Pile one-quarter of the mixture on each baked custard. Return to the oven for 5 minutes. Stand 5 minutes before serving.

Preparation Time: 5 minutes
Cooking Time: 35 minutes
Serves 4

Cook's tip

Caster sugar is best when making meringues as it dissolves during beating, giving you a smooth, glossy meringue topping.

Preparation Time: 15 minutes
Cooking Time: 20 minutes
Serves 4

Cook's tip

In place of pears, try **Wattie's**
Peach Slices or **Wattie's**
Apricot Halves. A nice change
to just cream or yoghurt is to
mix the two together. Whip ½
cup of cream until light and
fold in ½ cup of your favourite
yoghurt. This mixture combines
the velvety richness of cream
with the freshness of yoghurt.

*Here's the heart template for you to use as a guide. Trace
onto baking paper, cut it out, making it larger as you go.*

pear hearts
with
apricot glaze

Simple desserts are the order of the day. With a can of fruit and pre-rolled sheets of pastry, it's easy to make variations on a tart or pie theme. These heart shaped pear tarts are fabulous for younger members of the family to make – they can decorate them up as they wish. Don't forget to glaze with warmed apricot jam before serving. The pears will look just great.

Ingredients

2 sheets pre-rolled puff pastry, defrosted

2 tblsp sultanas

*1 tblsp **Craig's Apricot Jam***

*410 gram can **Wattie's Pear Quarters**, well drained*

milk to glaze

*2 tblsp **Craig's Apricot Jam**, to glaze*

icing sugar to dust

Method

1 Cut each pastry sheet in half.

2 Cut a heart shape from each half. The easiest way to do this is to fold the sheet in half and cut one half from the join, so when you open it out you have a whole heart.

3 Mix the sultanas with the one tablespoon jam and place a spoonful in the centre of each heart. Arrange about 3 pear quarters on top.

4 Cut strips from the leftover pieces of pastry and arrange on top crossed over. Then use any remaining pieces to decorate the hearts with.

5 Brush with milk to glaze. Place on a greased baking tray. Bake at 220°C for 15-20 minutes until the pastry is golden.

6 Heat 2 tablespoons jam in the microwave and spread on top of the pears when you remove them from the oven to give a golden glaze. Dust with sifted icing sugar to serve. Serve hot with whipped cream or yoghurt.

quick
trifle

This trifle recipe was a smash hit with viewers. It's the ultimate 'no-work, no-cook' dessert and proved to be just the thing for summer. I like to leave the trifle overnight or for at least four hours before topping with cream so that the sherry really has time to soak in with the other ingredients. Top with the whipped cream before serving if you do this.

Ingredients

1 half of a double sponge

about 4 tblsp **Craig's Raspberry Jam**

½ cup sweet or medium-sweet sherry

410 gram can **Wattie's Fruit Salad in Light Syrup***, well drained*

300 ml bottle cream

600 ml carton prepared vanilla custard

To Garnish
¼ cup grated chocolate

Method

1 Spread sponge with the raspberry jam and place in the base and sides of a large serving bowl.

2 Pour over the sherry. A splash more won't hurt.

3 Spread the well-drained fruit salad on top.

4 Whip the cream until soft peaks form and blend half the whipped cream with the custard. Spread the custard evenly over the fruit and sponge.

5 Spread the remaining whipped cream over the top of the custard and refrigerate one hour before serving. Decorate with grated chocolate before serving.

This is the team. Mike O'Sullivan and wife Melanie (right), Warwick and I, and my right-hand lady Anna Richards (left) in the final throws of checking the book before it goes off to the printer and catching any last photographs with Alan Gillard. We hope you've enjoyed the book as much as we did putting it together.

Preparation Time: 30 minutes
Standing Time: At least 1 hour
Serves 8

Cook's tip

If you ever have whipped or pouring cream that's a day or two past its 'best use date', don't throw it out, use it to make scones or pikelets.

index